Explorations
An Anthology of Literature

Volume A

Editor: John Holdren

Project Manager: Corey Maender

Text Editor: Joel Storer

Rights Specialist: Jean Stringer

Art Director: Suzanne Montazer

Design and Illustration: Stephanie Shaw

Production Manager: Lisa Dimaio Iekel

ISBN: 1–60153–025–0

Printed by Worzalla, Stevens Point, WI, USA, March 2012, Lot 032012

TABLE OF CONTENTS

STORIES OF OUR TIME

TO EVERYTHING THERE IS A SEASON

Stories of Scientists

Advice and Instruction

STORIES OF
OUR TIME

THANK YOU, M'AM

Langston Hughes

She was a large woman with a large purse that had everything in it but a hammer and nails. It had a long strap, and she carried it slung across her shoulder. It was about eleven o'clock at night, dark, and she was walking alone, when a boy ran up behind her and tried to snatch her purse. The strap broke with the sudden single tug the boy gave it from behind. But the boy's weight and the weight of the purse combined caused him to lose his balance. Instead of taking off full blast as he had hoped, the boy fell on his back on the sidewalk and his legs flew up. The large woman simply turned around and kicked him right square in his blue-jeaned sitter. Then she reached down, picked the boy up by his shirt front, and shook him until his teeth rattled.

After that the woman said, "Pick up my pocketbook, boy, and give it here."

She still held him tightly. But she bent down enough to permit him to stoop and pick up her purse. Then she said, "Now ain't you ashamed of yourself?"

Firmly gripped by his shirt front, the boy said, "Yes'm."

The woman said, "What did you want to do it for?"

The boy said, "I didn't aim to."

She said, "You a lie!"

By that time two or three people passed, stopped, turned to look, and some stood watching.

"If I turn you loose, will you run?" asked the woman.

"Yes'm," said the boy.

"Then I won't turn you loose," said the woman. She did not release him.

"Lady, I'm sorry," whispered the boy.

"Um-hum! Your face is dirty. I got a great mind to wash your face for you. Ain't you got nobody home to tell you to wash your face?"

"No'm," said the boy.

"Then it will get washed this evening," said the large woman, starting up the street, dragging the frightened boy behind her.

He looked as if he were fourteen or fifteen, frail and willow-wild, in tennis shoes and blue jeans.

The woman said, "You ought to be my son. I would teach you right from wrong. Least I can do right now is to wash your face. Are you hungry?"

"No'm," said the being-dragged boy. "I just want you to turn me loose."

"Was I bothering you when I turned that corner?" asked the woman.

"No'm."

"But you put yourself in contact with me?" said the woman. "If you think that that contact is not going to last awhile, you got another thought coming. When I get through with you, sir, you are going to remember Mrs. Luella Bates Washington Jones."

Sweat popped out on the boy's face and he began to struggle. Mrs. Jones stopped, jerked him around in front of her, put a half nelson about his neck, and continued to drag him up the street. When she got to her door, she dragged the boy inside, down a hall, and into a large kitchenette-furnished room at the rear of the house. She switched on the light and left the door open. The boy could hear other roomers laughing and talking in the large house. Some of their doors were open, too, so he knew he and the woman were not alone. The woman still had him by the neck in the middle of her room.

She said, "What is your name?"

"Roger," answered the boy.

"Then, Roger, you go to that sink and wash your face," said the woman, whereupon she turned him loose—at last. Roger looked at the door—looked at the woman—looked at the door—and went to the sink.

"Let the water run until it gets warm," she said. "Here's a clean towel."

"You gonna take me to jail?" asked the boy, bending over the sink.

"Not with that face, I would not take you nowhere," said the woman. "Here I am trying to get home to cook me a bite to eat, and you snatch my pocketbook! Maybe you ain't been to your supper either, late as it be. Have you?"

"There's nobody home at my house," said the boy.

"Then we'll eat," said the woman. "I believe you're hungry—or been hungry—to try to snatch my pocketbook!"

"I want a pair of blue suede shoes," said the boy.

"Well, you didn't have to snatch my pocketbook to get some suede shoes," said Mrs. Luella Bates Washington Jones. "You could of asked me."

"M'am?"

The water dripping from his face, the boy looked at her. There was a long pause. A very long pause. After he had dried his face and not knowing what else to do, dried it again, the boy turned around, wondering what next. The door was open. He could make a dash for it down the hall. He could run, run, run, *run!*

The woman was sitting on the daybed. After a while she said, "I were young once and I wanted things I could not get."

There was another long pause. The boy's mouth opened. Then he frowned, not knowing he frowned.

The woman said, "Um-hum! You thought I was going to say *but,* didn't you? You thought I was going to say, *but I didn't snatch people's pocketbooks.* Well, I wasn't going to say that." Pause. Silence. "I have done things, too, which I would not tell you, son—neither tell God, if He didn't already know. Everybody's got something in common. So you set down while I fix us something to eat. You might run that comb through your hair so you will look presentable."

In another corner of the room behind a screen was a gas plate and an icebox. Mrs. Jones got up and went behind the screen. The woman did not watch the boy to see if he was going to run now, nor did she watch her purse, which she left behind her on the daybed. But the boy took care to sit on the far side of the room,

---

presentable: worthy of being seen by others

away from the purse, where he thought she could easily see him out of the corner of her eye if she wanted to. He did not trust the woman not to trust him. And he did not want to be mistrusted now.

"Do you need somebody to go to the store," asked the boy, "maybe to get some milk or something?"

"Don't believe I do," said the woman, "unless you just want sweet milk yourself. I was going to make cocoa out of this canned milk I got here."

"That will be fine," said the boy.

She heated some lima beans and ham she had in the icebox, made the cocoa, and set the table. The woman did not ask the boy anything about where he lived, or his folks, or anything else that would embarrass him. Instead, as they ate, she told him about her job in a hotel beauty shop that stayed open late, what the work was like, and how all kinds of women came in and out, blondes, redheads, and Spanish. Then she cut him a half of her ten-cent cake.

"Eat some more, son," she said.

When they were finished eating, she got up and said, "Now here, take this ten dollars and buy yourself some blue suede shoes. And next time, do not make the mistake of latching onto my pocketbook nor nobody else's—because shoes got by devilish ways will burn your feet. I got to get my rest now. But from here on in, son, I hope you will behave yourself."

She led him down the hall to the front door and opened it. "Good night! Behave yourself, boy!" she said, looking out into the street as he went down the steps.

The boy wanted to say something other than, "Thank you, m'am," to Mrs. Luella Bates Washington Jones, but although his lips moved, he couldn't even say that as he turned at the foot of the barren stoop and looked up at the large woman in the door. Then she shut the door.

---

barren: bare

THE CIRCUIT

Francisco Jiménez

It was that time of year again. Ito, the strawberry sharecropper, did not smile. It was natural. The peak of the strawberry season was over and the last few days the workers, most of them braceros, were not picking as many boxes as they had during the months of June and July.

As the last days of August disappeared, so did the number of braceros. Sunday, only one—the best picker—came to work. I liked him. Sometimes we talked during our half-hour lunch break. That is how I found out he was from Jalisco, the same state in Mexico my family was from. That Sunday was the last time I saw him.

When the sun had tired and sunk behind the mountains, Ito signaled us that it was time to go home. "Ya esora," he yelled in his broken Spanish. Those were the words I waited for twelve hours a day, every day, seven days a week, week after week. And the thought of not hearing them again saddened me.

As we drove home Papá did not say a word. With both hands on the wheel, he stared at the dirt road. My older brother, Roberto, was also silent. He leaned his head back and closed his eyes. Once in a while he cleared from his throat the dust that blew in from outside.

Yes, it was that time of year. When I opened the front door to the shack, I stopped. Everything we owned was neatly packed in cardboard boxes. Suddenly I felt even more the weight of hours, days, weeks, and months of work. I sat down on a box. The thought of having to move to Fresno and knowing what was in store for me there brought tears to my eyes.

---

sharecropper: a farmer who rents land and uses a share of the crops to pay the rent
braceros: Mexican laborers who work seasonally on farms
Ya esora: Spanish for "It's time," or "Time's up."

That night I could not sleep. I lay in bed thinking about how much I hated this move.

A little before five o'clock in the morning, Papá woke everyone up. A few minutes later, the yelling and screaming of my little brothers and sisters, for whom the move was a great adventure, broke the silence of dawn. Shortly, the barking of the dogs accompanied them.

While we packed the breakfast dishes, Papá went outside to start the "Carcanchita." That was the name Papá gave his old '38 black Plymouth. He bought it in a used-car lot in Santa Rosa in the winter of 1949. Papá was very proud of his little jalopy. He had a right to be proud of it. He spent a lot of time looking at other cars before buying this one. When he finally chose the "Carcanchita," he checked it thoroughly before driving it out of the car lot. He examined every inch of the car. He listened to the motor, tilting his head from side to side like a parrot, trying to detect any noises that spelled car trouble. After being satisfied with the looks and sounds of the car, Papá then insisted on knowing who the original owner was. He never did find out from the car salesman, but he bought the car anyway. Papá figured the original owner must have been an important man because behind the rear seat of the car he found a blue necktie.

Papá parked the car out in front and left the motor running. "Listo," he yelled. Without saying a word, Roberto and I began to carry the boxes out to the car. Roberto carried the two big boxes and I carried the two smaller ones. Papá then threw the mattress on top of the car roof and tied it with ropes to the front and rear bumpers.

Everything was packed except Mamá's pot. It was an old large galvanized pot she had picked up at an army surplus store in Santa Maria the year I was born. The pot had many dents and nicks, and the more dents and nicks it acquired the more Mamá liked it. "Mi olla," she used to say proudly.

---

jalopy: an old, run-down car
listo: Spanish for "ready"
galvanized: coated with zinc
Mi olla: Spanish for "my kettle"

I held the front door open as Mamá carefully carried out her pot by both handles, making sure not to spill the cooked beans. When she got to the car, Papá reached out to help her with it. Roberto opened the rear car door and Papá gently placed it on the floor behind the front seat. All of us then climbed in. Papá sighed, wiped the sweat off his forehead with his sleeve, and said wearily: "Es todo."

As we drove away, I felt a lump in my throat. I turned around and looked at our little shack for the last time.

At sunset we drove into a labor camp near Fresno. Since Papá did not speak English, Mamá asked the camp foreman if he needed any more workers. "We don't need no more," said the foreman, scratching his head. "Check with Sullivan down the road. Can't miss him. He lives in a big white house with a fence around it."

When we got there, Mamá walked up to the house. She went through a white gate, past a row of rose bushes, up the stairs to the front door. She rang the doorbell. The porch light went on and a tall husky man came out. They exchanged a few words. After the man went in, Mamá clasped her hands and hurried back to the car. "We have work! Mr. Sullivan said we can stay there the whole season," she said, gasping and pointing to an old garage near the stables.

The garage was worn out by the years. It had no windows. The walls, eaten by termites, strained to support the roof full of holes. The dirt floor, populated by earthworms, looked like a gray road map.

That night, by the light of a kerosene lamp, we unpacked and cleaned our new home. Roberto swept away the loose dirt, leaving the hard ground. Papá plugged the holes in the walls with old newspapers and tin can tops. Mamá fed my little brothers and sisters. Papá and Roberto then brought in the mattress and placed it in the far corner of the garage. "Mamá, you and the little ones sleep on the mattress. Roberto, Panchito, and I will sleep outside under the trees," Papá said.

Es todo: Spanish for "That's everything."
husky: big and burly

Early next morning Mr. Sullivan showed us where his crop was, and after breakfast, Papá, Roberto, and I headed for the vineyard to pick.

Around nine o'clock the temperature had risen to almost one hundred degrees. I was completely soaked in sweat and my mouth felt as if I had been chewing on a handkerchief. I walked over to the end of the row, picked up the jug of water we had brought, and began drinking. "Don't drink too much; you'll get sick," Roberto shouted. No sooner had he said that than I felt sick to my stomach. I dropped to my knees and let the jug roll off my hands. I remained motionless with my eyes glued on the hot sandy ground. All I could hear was the drone of insects. Slowly I began to recover. I poured water over my face and neck and watched the dirty water run down my arms to the ground.

I still felt a little dizzy when we took a break to eat lunch. It was past two o'clock and we sat underneath a large walnut tree that was on the side of the road. While we ate, Papá jotted down the number of boxes we had picked. Roberto drew designs on the ground with a stick. Suddenly I noticed Papá's face turn pale as he looked down the road. "Here comes the school bus," he whispered loudly in alarm. Instinctively, Roberto and I ran and hid in the vineyards. We did not want to get in trouble for not going to school. The neatly dressed boys about my age got off. They carried books under their arms. After they crossed the street, the bus drove away. Roberto and I came out from hiding and joined Papá. "Tienen que tener cuidado," he warned us.

After lunch we went back to work. The sun kept beating down. The buzzing insects, the wet sweat, and the hot dry dust made the afternoon seem to last forever. Finally the mountains around the valley reached out and swallowed the sun. Within an hour it was too dark to continue picking. The vines blanketed the grapes, making it difficult to see the bunches. "Vamonos," said Papá,

---

instinctively: naturally; spontaneously
Tienen que tener cuidado: Spanish for "You have to be careful."
Vamonos: Spanish for "Let's go."

signaling to us that it was time to quit work. Papá then took out a pencil and began to figure out how much we had earned our first day. He wrote down numbers, crossed some out, wrote down some more. "Quince," he murmured.

When we arrived home, we took a cold shower underneath a waterhose. We then sat down to eat dinner around some wooden crates that served as a table. Mamá had cooked a special meal for us. We had rice and tortillas with "carne con chile," my favorite dish.

The next morning I could hardly move. My body ached all over. I felt little control over my arms and legs. This feeling went on every morning for days until my muscles finally got used to the work.

It was Monday, the first week of November. The grape season was over and I could now go to school. I woke up early that morning and lay in bed, looking at the stars and savoring the thought of not going to work and of starting sixth grade for the first time that year. Since I could not sleep, I decided to get up and join Papá and Roberto at breakfast. I sat at the table across from Roberto, but I kept my head down. I did not want to look up and face him. I knew he was sad. He was not going to school today. He was not going tomorrow, or next week, or next month. He would not go until the cotton season was over, and that was sometime in February. I rubbed my hands together and watched the dry, acid stained skin fall to the floor in little rolls.

When Papá and Roberto left for work, I felt relief. I walked to the top of a small grade next to the shack and watched the "Carcanchita" disappear in the distance in a cloud of dust.

Two hours later, around eight o'clock, I stood by the side of the road waiting for school bus number twenty. When it arrived I climbed in. Everyone was busy either talking or yelling. I sat in an empty seat in the back.

When the bus stopped in front of the school, I felt very nervous. I looked out the bus window and saw boys and girls carrying books under their arms. I put my hands in my pant pockets and walked to the principal's office. When I entered I heard a woman's voice

---

quince: Spanish for "fifteen"
carne con chile: a spicy dish of meat with beans
savoring: deeply enjoying

say: "May I help you?" I was startled. I had not heard English for months. For a few seconds I remained speechless. I looked at the lady who waited for an answer. My first instinct was to answer her in Spanish, but I held back. Finally, after struggling for English words, I managed to tell her that I wanted to enroll in the sixth grade. After answering many questions, I was led to the classroom.

Mr. Lema, the sixth grade teacher, greeted me and assigned me a desk. He then introduced me to the class. I was so nervous and scared at that moment when everyone's eyes were on me that I wished I were with Papá and Roberto picking cotton. After taking roll, Mr. Lema gave the class the assignment for the first hour. "The first thing we have to do this morning is finish reading the story we began yesterday," he said enthusiastically. He walked up to me, handed me an English book, and asked me to read. "We are on page 125," he said politely. When I heard this, I felt my blood rush to my head; I felt dizzy. "Would you like to read?" he asked hesitantly. I opened the book to page 125. My mouth was dry. My eyes began to water. I could not begin. "You can read later," Mr. Lema said understandingly.

For the rest of the reading period I kept getting angrier and angrier with myself. I should have read, I thought to myself.

During recess I went into the restroom and opened my English book to page 125. I began to read in a low voice pretending I was in class. There were many words I did not know. I closed the book and headed back to the classroom.

Mr. Lema was sitting at his desk correcting papers. When I entered he looked up at me and smiled. I felt better. I walked up to him and asked if he could help me with the new words. "Gladly," he said.

The rest of the month I spent my lunch hours working on English with Mr. Lema, my best friend at school.

One Friday during lunch hour Mr. Lema asked me to take a walk with him to the music room. "Do you like music?" he asked me as we entered the building.

"Yes, I like corridos," I answered. He then picked up a trumpet, blew on it and handed it to me. The sound gave me goose bumps.

corridos: traditional Mexican and Mexican-American songs that tell stories

I knew that sound. I had heard it in many corridos. "How would you like to learn how to play it?" he asked. He must have read my face because before I could answer, he added: "I'll teach you how to play it during our lunch hours."

That day I could hardly wait to get home to tell Papá and Mamá the great news. As I got off the bus, my little brothers and sisters ran up to meet me. They were yelling and screaming. I thought they were happy to see me, but when I opened the door to our shack, I saw that everything we owned was neatly packed in cardboard.

THE BRACELET

Yoshiko Uchida

"**M**ama, is it time to go?" I hadn't planned to cry, but the tears came suddenly and I wiped them away with the back of my hand. I didn't want my older sister to see me crying.

"It's almost time, Ruri," my mother said gently. Her face was filled with a kind of sadness I had never seen before.

I looked around at the empty room. The clothes Mama always told me to hang up in the closet, the junk piled on my dresser, the old rag doll I could never bear to part with—they were all gone. There was nothing left in my room, and there was nothing left in the rest of the house. The rugs and furniture were gone, the pictures and drapes were down, and the closets and cupboards were empty. The house was like a gift box after the nice thing inside was gone; just a lot of nothingness.

It was almost time to leave our home, but we weren't moving to a nicer house or to a new town. It was April 21, 1942. The United States and Japan were at war, and every Japanese person on the West Coast was being evacuated by the government to a concentration camp. Mama, my sister Keiko, and I were being sent from our home, and out of Berkeley, and eventually out of California.

The doorbell rang, and I ran to answer it before my sister could. I thought maybe by some miracle a messenger from the government might be standing there, tall and proper and buttoned into a uniform, come to tell us it was all a terrible mistake, that we wouldn't have to leave after all. Or maybe the messenger would have a telegram from Papa, who was interned in a prisoner-of-war camp in Montana because he had worked for a Japanese business firm.

---

evacuated: removed; withdrawn
telegram: a message sent electronically over telegraph wires
interned: confined; held

The FBI had come to pick up Papa and hundreds of other Japanese community leaders on the very day that Japanese planes had bombed Pearl Harbor. The government thought they were dangerous enemy aliens. If it weren't so sad, it would have been funny. Papa could no more be dangerous than the mayor of our city, and he was every bit as loyal to the United States. He had lived here since 1917.

When I opened the door, it wasn't a messenger from anywhere. It was my best friend, Laurie Madison, from next door. She was holding a package wrapped up like a birthday present, and she wasn't wearing her party dress, and her face drooped like a wilted tulip.

"Hi," she said. "I came to say goodbye."

She thrust the present at me and told me it was something to take to camp. "It's a bracelet," she said before I could open the package. "Put it on so you won't have to pack it." She knew I didn't have one inch of space left in my suitcase. We had been instructed to take only what we could carry into camp, and Mama had told us we could each take only two suitcases.

"Then how are we ever going to pack the dishes and blankets and sheets they've told us to bring with us?" Keiko worried.

"I don't really know," Mama had said, and she simply began packing those big impossible things into an enormous duffle bag, along with umbrellas, boots, a kettle, hot plate, and flashlight.

"Who's going to carry that huge sack?" I asked.

But Mama didn't worry about things like that. "Someone will help us," she said. "Don't worry." So I didn't.

Laurie wanted me to open her package and put the bracelet on before she left. It was a thin gold chain with a heart dangling on it. She helped me put it on, and I told her I'd never take it off, ever.

"Well, goodbye then," Laurie said awkwardly. "Come home soon."

"I will," I said, although I didn't know if I would ever get back to Berkeley again.

---

aliens: people from a foreign country
wilted: drooping from lack of water

I watched Laurie go down the block, her long blond pigtails bouncing as she walked. I wondered who'd be sitting in my desk at Lincoln Junior High now that I was gone. Laurie kept turning and waving, even walking backward for a while, until she got to the corner. I didn't want to watch anymore, and I slammed the door shut.

The next time the doorbell rang, it was Mrs. Simpson, our other neighbor. She was going to drive us to the Congregational Church, which was the Civil Control Station where all the Japanese of Berkeley were supposed to report.

It was time to go. "Come on, Ruri. Get your things," my sister called to me.

It was a warm day, but I put on a sweater and my coat so I wouldn't have to carry them and I picked up my two suitcases. Each one had a tag with my name and our family number on it. Every Japanese family had to register and get a number. We were Family Number 13453.

Mama was taking one last look around our house. She was going from room to room, as though she were trying to take a mental picture of the house she had lived in for fifteen years, so she would never forget it.

I saw her take a long last look at the garden that Papa loved. The irises beside the fish pond were just beginning to bloom. If Papa had been home, he would have cut the first iris blossom and brought it inside to Mama. "This one is for you," he would have said. And Mama would have smiled and said, "Thank you, Papa San," and put it in her favorite cut-glass vase.

But the garden looked shabby and forsaken now that Papa was gone and Mama was too busy to take care of it. It looked the way I felt, sort of empty and lonely and abandoned.

When Mrs. Simpson took us to the Civil Control Station, I felt even worse. I was scared, and for a minute I thought I was going to lose my breakfast right in front of everybody. There must have been over a thousand Japanese people gathered at the church.

---

forsaken: abandoned

Some were old and some were young. Some were talking and laughing, and some were crying. I guess everybody else was scared too. No one knew exactly what was going to happen to us. We just knew that we were being taken to the Tanforan Racetracks, which the army had turned into a camp for the Japanese. There were fourteen other camps like ours along the West Coast.

What scared me the most were the soldiers standing at the doorway of the church hall. They were carrying guns with mounted bayonets. I wondered if they thought we would try to run away and whether they'd shoot us or come after us with their bayonets if we did.

A long line of buses waited to take us to camp. There were trucks too, for our baggage. And Mama was right; some men were there to help us load our duffel bag. When it was time to board the buses, I sat with Keiko, and Mama sat behind us. The bus went down Grove Street and passed the small Japanese food store where Mama used to order her bean-curd cakes and pickled radish. The windows were all boarded up, but there was a sign still hanging on the door that read, "We are loyal Americans."

The crazy thing about the whole evacuation was that we were all loyal Americans. Most of us were citizens because we had been born here. But our parents, who had come from Japan, couldn't become citizens because there was a law that prevented any Asian from becoming a citizen. Now everybody with a Japanese face was being shipped off to concentration camps.

"It's stupid," Keiko muttered as we saw the racetrack looming up beside the highway. "If there were any Japanese spies around, they'd have gone back to Japan long ago."

"I'll say," I agreed. My sister was in high school and she ought to know, I thought.

When the bus turned in to Tanforan, there were even more armed guards at the gate, and I saw barbed wire strung around the entire grounds. I felt as though I were going into a prison, but I hadn't done anything wrong.

---

bayonets: blades attached to the ends of rifles
evacuation: the removal of a group of people

We streamed off the buses and poured into a huge room, where doctors looked down our throats and peeled back our eyelids to see if we had any diseases. Then we were given our housing assignments. The man in charge gave Mama a slip of paper. We were in Barrack 16, Apartment 40.

"Mama!" I said. "We're going to live in an apartment!" The only apartment I had ever seen was the one my piano teacher lived in. It was an enormous building in San Francisco, with an elevator and thick carpeted hallways. I thought how wonderful it would be to have our own elevator. A house was all right, but an apartment seemed elegant and special.

We walked down the racetrack, looking for Barrack 16. Mr. Noma, a friend of Papa's, helped us carry our bags. I was so busy looking around I slipped and almost fell on the muddy track. Army barracks had been built everywhere, all around the racetrack and even in the center oval.

Mr. Noma pointed beyond the track toward the horse stables. "I think your barrack is out there."

He was right. We came to a long stable that had once housed the horses of Tanforan, and we climbed up the wide ramp. Each stall had a number painted on it, and when we got to number 40, Mr. Noma pushed open the door.

"Well, here it is," he said, "Apartment 40." The stall was narrow and empty and dark. There were two small windows on each side of the door. Three folded army cots were on the dust-covered floor, and one light bulb dangled from the ceiling. That was all. This was our apartment, and it still smelled like horses.

Mama looked at my sister and then at me. "It won't be so bad when we fix it up," she began. "I'll ask Mr. Simpson to send me some materials for curtains. I could make some cushions too, and... well..." She stopped. She couldn't think of anything more to say.

Mr. Noma said he'd go get some mattresses for us. "I'd better hurry before they're all gone." He rushed off. I think he wanted to leave so that he wouldn't have to see Mama cry. But he needn't have run off, because Mama didn't cry. She just went out to borrow a broom and began sweeping out the dust and dirt. "Will you girls set up the cots?" she asked.

It was only after we'd put up the last cot that I noticed my bracelet was gone. "I've lost Laurie's bracelet!" I screamed. "My bracelet's gone!"

We looked all over the stall and even down the ramp. I wanted to run back down to the track and go over every inch of ground we'd walked on, but it was getting dark and Mama wouldn't let me.

I thought of what I'd promised Laurie. I wasn't ever going to take the bracelet off, not even when I went to take a shower. And now I had lost it on my very first day in camp. I wanted to cry.

I kept looking for it all the time we were in Tanforan. I didn't stop looking until the day we were sent to another camp called Topaz, in the middle of a desert in Utah. And then I gave up.

But Mama told me never mind. She said I didn't need a bracelet to remember Laurie, just as I didn't need anything to remember Papa or our home in Berkeley or all the people and things we loved and had left behind.

"Those are things we can carry in our hearts and take with us no matter where we are sent," she said.

And I guess she was right. I've never forgotten Laurie, even now.

To Everything There Is a Season

Waiting

Harry Behn

Dreaming of honeycombs to share
With her small cubs, a mother bear
Sleeps in a snug and snowy lair.

Bees in the drowsy, drifted hive
Sip hoarded honey to survive
Until the flowers come alive.

Sleeping beneath the deep snow
Seeds of honeyed flowers know
When it is time to wake and grow.

lair: the home of a wild animal
hoarded: saved up, stored away

SOMETHING TOLD
THE WILD GEESE

Rachel Field

Something told the wild geese
    It was time to go.
Though the fields lay golden
    Something whispered, "Snow."
Leaves were green and stirring,
    Berries, luster-glossed,
But beneath warm feathers
    Something cautioned, "Frost."
All the sagging orchards
    Steamed with amber spice,
But each wild breast stiffened
    At remembered ice.
Something told the wild geese
    It was time to fly—
Summer sun was on their wings,
    Winter in their cry.

luster-glossed: shiny with light
amber: a warm, yellow-brown color

Six Haiku

translated by Harry Behn

Broken and broken
again on the sea, the moon
so easily mends.

–Chosu

Watching the full moon,
a small hungry boy forgets
to eat his supper.

–Basho

Behind me the moon
brushes a shadow of pines
lightly on the floor.

–Kikaku

Out of the sky, geese
come honking in the spring's cold
early-morning light.

—*Soin*

O foolish ducklings,
you know my old green pond is
watched by a weasel!

—*Buson*

A spark in the sun,
this tiny flower has roots
deep in the cool earth.

—*Harry Behn*

CHECK

James Stephens

The Night was creeping on the ground!
She crept and did not make a sound,

Until she reached the tree: And then
She covered it, and stole again

Along the grass beside the wall!
—I heard the rustling of her shawl

As she threw blackness everywhere
Along the sky, the ground, the air,

And in the room where I was hid!
But, no matter what she did

To everything that was without,
She could not put my candle out!

So I stared at the Night! And she
Stared back solemnly at me!

---

solemnly: seriously and sternly

THE PASTURE

Robert Frost

I'm going out to clean the pasture spring;
I'll only stop to rake the leaves away
(And wait to watch the clear water, I may):
I shan't be gone long.—You come too.

I'm going out to fetch the little calf
That's standing by the mother. It's so young
It totters when she licks it with her tongue.
I shan't be gone long.—You come too.

shan't: contraction for "shall not"
totters: stands unsteadily; wobbles

A Wintry Sonnet

Christina Rossetti

A Robin said: The Spring will never come,
    And I shall never care to build again.
A Rosebush said: These frosts are wearisome,
    My sap will never stir for sun or rain.
The half Moon said: These nights are fogged and slow,
    I neither care to wax nor care to wane.
The Ocean said: I thirst from long ago,
    Because earth's rivers cannot fill the main.—
When Springtime came, red Robin built a nest,
    And trilled a lover's song in sheer delight.
Grey hoarfrost vanished, and the Rose with might
    Clothed her in leaves and buds of crimson core.
The dim Moon brightened. Ocean sunned his crest,
    Dimpled his blue,—yet thirsted evermore.

---

wearisome: tiring
trilled: sang
hoarfrost: frost
crimson: dark red

The Morns Are Meeker Than They Were

Emily Dickinson

The morns are meeker than they were—
The nuts are getting brown—
The berry's cheek is plumper—
The Rose is out of town.

The Maple wears a gayer scarf—
The field a scarlet gown—
Lest I should be old fashioned
I'll put a trinket on.

meeker: milder; gentler
gayer: brighter; more cheerful
scarlet: bright red
lest: for fear that
trinket: a small ornament, such as piece of jewelry

THE STORM

Walter de la Mare

First there were two of us, then there were three of us,
Then there was one bird more,
Four of us—wild white sea-birds,
Treading the ocean floor;
And the wind rose, and the sea rose,
To the angry billows' roar—
With one of us—two of us—three of us—four of us
Sea-birds on the shore.

Soon there were five of us, soon there were nine of us,
And lo! in a trice sixteen!
And the yeasty surf curdled over the sands,
The gaunt gray rocks between;
And the tempest raved, and the lightning's fire
Struck blue on the spindrift hoar—
And on four of us—ay, and on four times four of us
Sea-birds on the shore.

---

billows: large waves
in a trice: an expression meaning "in an instant"
yeasty: bubbly like yeast
gaunt: barren
tempest: a wild storm
spindrift: sea spray
hoar: from hoary = gray or white

And our sixteen waxed to thirty-two,
And they to past three score—
A wild, white welter of winnowing wings,
And ever more and more;
And the winds lulled, and the seas went down,
And the sun streamed out on high,
Gilding the pools and the spume and the spars
'Neath the vast blue deeps of the sky;

And the isles and the bright green headlands shone,
As they'd never shone before,
Mountains and valleys of silver cloud,
Wherein to swing, sweep, soar—
A host of screeching, scolding, scrabbling
Sea-birds on the shore—
A snowy, silent, sun-washed drift
Of sea birds on the shore.

---

waxed: increased
score: twenty
welter: state of confusion; chaos
winnowing: blowing; fanning
lulled: calmed down
gilding: turning a golden color
spume: foam
spars: poles that support the rigging (ropes) of a sailing ship
isles: islands

Swift Things Are Beautiful

Elizabeth Coatsworth

Swift things are beautiful:
Swallows and deer,
And lightning that falls
Bright-veined and clear,
Rivers and meteors,
Wind in the wheat,
The strong-withered horse,
The runner's sure feet.

And slow things are beautiful:
The closing of day,
The pause of the wave
That curves downward to spray,
The ember that crumbles,
The opening flower,
And the ox that moves on
In the quiet of power.

---

strong-withered: strong backed (*withers* are the highest part of a horse's back)
ember: a glowing coal

I Wandered Lonely as a Cloud

William Wordsworth

I wandered lonely as a cloud
    That floats on high o'er vales and hills,
When all at once I saw a crowd,—
    A host of golden daffodils
Beside the lake, beneath the trees,
Fluttering and dancing in the breeze.

Continuous as the stars that shine
    And twinkle on the Milky Way,
They stretched in never-ending line
    Along the margin of a bay:
Ten thousand saw I, at a glance,
Tossing their heads in sprightly dance.

The waves beside them danced, but they
    Outdid the sparkling waves in glee;
A poet could not but be gay
    In such a jocund company;
I gazed—and gazed—but little thought
What wealth the show to me had brought.

For oft, when on my couch I lie,
    In vacant or in pensive mood,
They flash upon that inward eye
    Which is the bliss of solitude;
And then my heart with pleasure fills,
And dances with the daffodils.

---

vales: valleys
host: a great many
margin: edge
sprightly: spirited; lively
glee: joy; delight
jocund: merry; happy

oft: often
vacant: without activity
pensive: thoughtful
bliss: joy; great happiness
solitude: the state of being alone

Until I Saw the Sea

Lilian Moore

Until I saw the sea
I did not know
that wind
could wrinkle water so.

I never knew
that sun
could splinter a whole sea of blue.

Nor
did I know before
a sea breathes in and out
upon a shore.

splinter: to split into thin pieces

"To everything there is a season"

Ecclesiastes 3:1-8; King James Bible

To everything there is a season, and a time for every
    purpose under heaven:
A time to be born, and a time to die; a time to plant,
    and a time to pluck up what is planted.
A time to kill, and a time to heal; a time to break down,
    and a time to build up;
A time to weep, and a time to laugh; a time to mourn,
    and a time to dance;
A time to cast away stones, and a time to gather stones together;
    a time to embrace, and a time to refrain from embracing;
A time to get, and a time to lose; a time to keep,
    and a time to cast away;
A time to rend, and a time to sew; a time to keep silence,
    and a time to speak;
A time to love, and a time to hate; a time of war,
    and a time of peace.

refrain: to keep from doing; to hold back
rend: to rip apart

STORIES OF
SCIENTISTS

The heights by great men reached and kept
Were not attained by sudden flight;
But they, while their companions slept,
Were toiling upward through the night.

—Henry Wadsworth Longfellow

Michael Faraday's World

Nancy Veglahn

I

Michael Faraday was always asking questions. He asked so many questions because he wondered about everything. He wondered what makes people sneeze, and whether flies have bones, and why candles burn, and what keeps the stars in order. It was not easy to get answers to questions like these in Michael Faraday's part of London in the beginning of the nineteenth century. But he kept asking and wondering.

When his father heated the blacksmith's forge, Michael wondered why the iron horseshoe nails became soft when they were heated, but the anvil didn't. When his mother baked bread, he wondered how the little bit of yeast she put in the dough could make the whole loaf rise. Most of all, Michael wondered why nobody else seemed to wonder as he did. His parents were too busy wondering how to get enough money to feed their four children and pay the bills.

When he was ten years old, Michael became an errand boy for a bookbinder, Mr. Riebau. Michael also had to sweep the floors, wash the windows, and keep things tidy. He liked working in the bookbinder's shop. He liked the smells of ink and glue and leather and crisp new paper. He liked Mr. Riebau. Most of all, he liked to read.

Sometimes Michael found articles about new inventions and scientific discoveries. He read these very carefully and thought about the people who figure out how things work.

---

bookbinder: a person who sews pages and covers together to make a book

Several older boys worked in Mr. Riebau's shop and lived in his house. They were called apprentices. These boys would work for the bookbinder for seven years; then they had learned enough to become bookbinders themselves. Michael watched them helping Mr. Riebau put new covers on worn-out books. Of course, he asked a lot of questions.

One day when Michael was fourteen years old, Mr. Riebau asked him a question. "You seem to like watching us work. Wouldn't you like to move here and be an apprentice?"

Michael Faraday lived and worked at Mr. Riebau's shop for seven years. Mr. Riebau let Michael read before work, after work, at mealtime—whenever there was a spare moment. He read everything that was sent to Mr. Riebau for binding: Arabian Nights, the plays of Shakespeare, a book of sermons, a history of England, nursery rhymes, scientific studies.

One day, Michael had a chance to read the "E" volume of the Encyclopedia Britannica. There was not time to read all of it, of course. The book would only be in Mr. Riebau's shop for a few days. He had to skip over sections like "Egg" and "Egret" and "Elamite."

But when he came to the article on "Electricity," Michael read every word. That took him several hours, because it was 127 pages long. He copied much of the information into his notebook. Electricity was one of the things Michael had wondered most about.

Mr. Riebau agreed to let Michael use the back of the shop at night for scientific experiments. He also let Michael have scraps of metal, wood, and glass, and bits of glue left over from bookbinding.

The shop was quiet at night. It was a good time to work and think. Michael built up the fire in the fireplace and used it to heat chemicals and melt metals. Shadows danced on the walls and ceilings as he worked. Sometimes one of his concoctions went wrong and exploded with a "pop." Usually by the time he dragged himself up the stairs to bed he had learned something, even if it was only what not to try again.

---

apprentices: people who are learning a trade from an expert
egret: a kind of bird like a heron
Elamite: an ancient language
concoctions: unusual mixtures

One day Mr. Riebau was talking to a wealthy customer, a Mr. Dance, about some new scientific books. "I have a boy here who'll want to read those," Mr. Riebau said, and told Mr. Dance about his curious apprentice. He called Michael into the room.

"Have you ever gone to hear the lectures at the Royal Institution?" Mr. Dance asked.

Michael shook his head.

"A boy with your interests shouldn't miss those. Sir Humphry Davy is speaking in a few weeks."

Michael knew that Sir Humphry Davy was the greatest scientist in England, and that the Royal Institution was the place where Davy and many other scientists did their work. He also knew the lectures cost money.

Mr. Dance must have understood Michael's problem, because a few days later he came back to the bookbinder's shop with tickets to four lectures by Sir Humphry Davy.

II

It was February, 1812. Napoleon's armies had conquered most of Europe. British soldiers were fighting the French in Spain and the Americans across the Atlantic. Michael Faraday knew all this, but he thought of nothing but the lectures.

On the night of the first lecture, he walked through lightly falling snow to Number 21 Albemarle Street. The Royal Institution was a large building of gray stone with fourteen pillars across the front. It looked as wonderful as a castle from the Arabian Nights, and as Michael walked up the wide stairs inside he felt sure there were amazing secrets hidden behind each closed door.

He found a seat in the crowded lecture hall, and soon Sir Humphry Davy appeared on the platform. As the great man spoke, Michael wrote down everything. His fingers ached, and his eyes burned from writing in the dimly lit room. He had no time to think about all the facts and theories Davy talked about. He would do that later.

In the next few weeks Michael copied the notes into a fresh notebook he had made. He drew pictures to show the equipment Davy had used on the platform and the experiments he had done.

There was another lecture in March and two in April. Michael took careful notes on all of them.

The finished notebook with its pictures was 386 pages long. It was full of facts about chemicals and gases and steam engines and the laws of nature.

But still Michael had questions. He had more questions than ever.

His years as Mr. Riebau's apprentice were almost over. In a few months he would be ready to go and work as a "journeyman" bookbinder. It was a good trade, and he liked it. Yet he could not forget the Royal Institution.

Faraday had a daring idea. Why not ask Sir Humphry whether there might be work for him at the Institution? Why not send him those lecture notes to show him that Michael Faraday could listen and learn? He put the notes in a neat package, included a letter, and sent the bundle to Sir Humphry Davy.

Months crawled by with no answer. Michael began to lose hope for the first time. He was twenty-two years old, a grown man with no money and no education except what he had found for himself. Maybe it was silly to dream of becoming a scientist.

One night early in 1813, Michael was getting ready for bed when he heard someone knocking loudly at the door. He looked out the window and saw a fancy carriage in the street. When he opened the door, he was even more startled to see a footman in a powdered wig and a coat with bright brass buttons. The man handed him a note. Michael was too surprised to say anything, and the footman got back into the carriage and drove away. Using a coal from the fire, Michael lit a candle and looked at the note. It was addressed to him.

Sir Humphry Davy wanted Michael Faraday to call the next morning at the Royal Institution.

After a sleepless night, Michael put on his best suit and walked to the big stone building in Albemarle Street. A doorman directed him to the office of Sir Humphry.

"I had to fire one of our laboratory assistants yesterday," Davy told him. "Got into a fight—the man was a troublemaker from the beginning. I need a helper to keep my equipment in order and write

---

journeyman: a person who has learned a trade but is not yet a master

up the records and perhaps even help me prepare for experiments. I remembered your letter and those amazing notes you took on my lectures...."

The salary would be a guinea a week, plus fuel, candles, and aprons. Best of all, Michael could live in the Royal Institution; there was a room available on the top floor. Michael made a bundle of his few extra clothes, his notebook, and other belongings. He left his homemade laboratory equipment behind; he would have better things to work with at the Royal Institution. A charwoman showed him to his room that evening. The roof slanted over his head, and the windows were small and dusty. All the furniture he needed was there: a narrow bed, a desk, some wooden chairs.

In the middle of the night, Michael was still awake, his heart thudding with excitement. He got up and lit a candle. Then he pulled his clothes on and crept down the stairs, through the wide hall, and into the laboratory where he was to work with Sir Humphry Davy.

Sir Humphry had shown the room to him earlier, but it looked different at night. The faint candle glow showed hints of the wonders of that room: gleaming glass jars and bright metal tools and mysterious chemicals stored on shelves that reached from floor to ceiling. A mixture of powerful smells made Michael's nose twitch. He would have to get used to all those chemical odors; they were even stronger than the smells of the bookbinding shop. A bit of hot wax stung his thumb. He looked down at the candle and wondered suddenly how it worked. He had been using candles all his life, but he had never noticed before that the flame was brighter at the top and bottom than in the middle. Why was that? He went back upstairs, climbed into bed, and fell asleep thinking about candles.

He started work in the wonderful laboratory the next morning. At first he only washed and dried the equipment and learned where everything was. But soon Sir Humphry let him help with the experiments themselves, and Michael began to feel like a scientist at last.

---

guinea: a gold coin once used in Britain
charwoman: a cleaning woman

He did so well as Davy's assistant that he was soon promoted to "Assistant and Superintendent of the Apparatus of the Laboratory and Mineralogical Collection." This long title meant that he could now do some of his own experiments as well as help the senior scientists.

III

It was an exciting time to be a scientist. All over the world discoveries were being made about the laws of nature. Each new discovery led to more experiments and more discoveries.

Michael Faraday was fascinated by magnets and electricity. He filled notebooks with accounts of experiments using magnets, wires, and batteries. Most of these experiments didn't work as he expected, but he kept trying.

He was not the only scientist trying to learn more about electricity. An Italian, Alessandro Volta, had discovered how to make a simple battery that produced small amounts of electricity from chemicals. A Frenchman, André Ampère, invented a device called a galvanometer, which could measure electric power. And in 1825, William Sturgeon made an electromagnet. He bent an iron bar into a horseshoe shape, wrapped it with copper wire, and sent an electric current through the wire. This turned the iron horseshoe into a powerful magnet that could hold as much as nine pounds of metal. As long as electric current went through the wire, the iron horseshoe was an electromagnet. When the current was turned off, it was just a piece of iron wrapped with wire.

Magnetism could be generated by electricity. And so, Michael Faraday wondered, why couldn't electricity be generated by magnetism?

No one was able to do it. Wires were wrapped around magnets in every possible way, but the magnets did not make any electric current.

---

apparatus: equipment
mineralogical: having to do with minerals

Faraday built a tiny model: an iron bar an inch long wrapped in a spiral of copper wire. He carried it in his vest pocket. When he was at a boring committee meeting or a long dinner party, he would take the model from his pocket and stare at it. What was the answer?

He believed that everything in the world worked together in ways that made sense, if people could only understand. The energy of lightning, of sparks, of magnetism and electricity, was the same energy in different forms. He was only trying to change the energy from one form to another.

One summer morning in 1831, Faraday sat at his workbench in the laboratory, writing down the story of another failure. He had wrapped a large bar-shaped magnet with wire, but nothing had happened. It didn't seem to matter how powerful the magnet was; it would not make an electric current.

Then he stopped and looked at the round lip of a glass beaker he was using. A circle! What if the magnet were round?

He had one of his helpers make a circle of soft iron. Faraday wrapped a coil of copper wire around one side of it. He called this Wire A. Around the other side of the ring he wrapped another wire, Wire B, which he attached to a galvanometer.

He then fastened Wire A to a small battery, sending an electrical charge through it, which made the iron ring into an electromagnet. He hoped that this would cause a current to flow in the second wire, the one that was not connected to the battery.

The needle on the galvanometer moved, showing a charge in Wire B. It fell back immediately, but the needle moved again when Faraday disconnected Wire A from the battery.

Faraday stared at the galvanometer. Had it moved showing an electric current in Wire B—or was he imagining it? He connected the battery to Wire A again; the needle moved again. But the moment he pulled the Wire A connection away, the needle fell back. It moved when he moved Wire A.

The experiment seemed to show that electricity could be generated from magnetism. But Faraday was not satisfied. As usual, the answer he found only raised more questions. Why wasn't the current steady? Why did the electrical charge in Wire B show up only when he connected or disconnected the battery to Wire A? Why did the needle always swing back?

Faraday spent the next three weeks thinking about it. He wrote in a letter to a friend, "I am busy just now again on electromagnetism, and think I have got hold of a good thing, but can't say."

He repeated the experiment, using wires and magnets in many different shapes and sizes. He discovered that all he had to do was to move an electromagnet close to a coil of wire and the needle would jump.

The important thing was motion! It was a moving magnet that could generate electric power. Faraday had his answer.

Many years later, this idea was used by others to build a machine called a dynamo. It is the dynamo that generates the power to run our modern washing machines and television sets and electric ovens. Faraday called the discovery that made the dynamo possible "magnetoelectric induction."

"But what's the use of it?" people would ask Faraday when he told them about making electric current from magnetism.

He liked to quote the answer Benjamin Franklin had given when asked a similar question: "What's the use of a baby?" Franklin had said. "Some day it will grow up."

IV

"Think about how wonderful it is to live, to stand up and move about." Michael Faraday looked from the stage of the auditorium of the Royal Institution to the rows and rows of young faces in the audience. "Yet most people don't wonder about these things. They might think a mountain was wonderful, or a waterfall, but not the fact that they can walk around in the daytime and lie down at night."

It was Christmastime. Faraday had started a new tradition at the Royal Institution. Every year during the Christmas holidays, he gave lectures about science to the children who were on vacation from school. They crowded into the auditorium to hear Faraday. Even the Prince of Wales, the future King of England, came to the Christmas lectures.

---

induction: the way in which a conductor receives an electrical current from a
magnetic field

Once Faraday put an ordinary candle on his desk and asked questions, just as he had always asked questions of everything. What makes a candle burn? Why is the flame always brighter toward the top? Where does the candle go when it has burned down to a stump? Why does its light go out if you put it under a glass jar? Why do some candles smoke a great deal and others very little?

Usually he told the children about some kind of experiment that they could do at home. After the lecture on candles, he told them to take a cold spoon and hold it over the flame of a candle. The spoon would then get a sort of mist over it. That showed that one of the products of a burning candle is water.

Sometimes Faraday had his desk piled with things the audience could take home and work with: bits of rock, pieces of wire, metals, and harmless chemicals. When he talked about static electricity, he told them how they could make a static electricity generator out of a piece of sealing wax, a watch, and a small wooden board.

One morning, as Faraday left the Royal Institution to take a walk through the cold, damp air, two young boys saw him and whispered to each other. Finally one of them said shyly, "Good morning, Mr. Faraday."

Michael Faraday smiled and said, "Good morning. May I ask how you gentlemen know my name?"

"We went to your Christmas lectures, sir," said the boy who had spoken before.

"All of them," the second boy grinned.

"We wondered if you'd tell us what the Christmas lectures will be about this year, sir," the first one said.

"I haven't decided yet," Faraday told them. "Perhaps they might have something to do with electricity."

"Oh, that would be first-rate!" said the second boy.

They thanked him and raced off, beaming. "Ask questions," he called after them. "Never stop asking questions!"

Nikola Tesla, Inventor

Shawn Lake

Nikola Tesla stood on the darkened stage with his hands on his hips and looked out at his audience. His white tuxedo seemed to shimmer in the dim light, and he was so tall and thin that he appeared to be walking on stilts. The year was 1891, and people filled every seat and stood in the aisles to listen to this elegant man with bright, blue eyes talk about electricity.

On tables nearby lay a dozen glass tubes that gave off an eerie glow. As Tesla stepped forward, the lights cast his shadow along the walls. He held up his hands to signal for silence. The audience leaned forward in their seats as he began to speak. In his careful, accented English, he told them about light bulbs and lightning, waterfalls and power, and how electricity was about to change everyone's future.

But Tesla had more than words in store for his audience. Taking hold of a wire, he spread his arms as tens of thousands of volts of electric power passed over his body. Streamers of blue light flowed over him, and sparks flew from his fingertips. When he picked up a long, glass tube, it began to glow. Tesla himself was the conductor of enough electricity to light up the bulb.

Nikola Tesla sounds like a nineteenth century sideshow performer, but he was one of the most brilliant inventors in history. In fact, every electrical appliance today uses at least one of Tesla's inventions.

If you had seen him striding down the street, though, you would never have thought that he spent most of his time building inventions in a laboratory. He looked more like a diplomat, with his tidy white shirt buttoned at the throat and his hair slicked back. If you had happened to sit by him in a restaurant, you would have

---

conductor: something that allows an electrical current to flow through it

thought he was a bit odd. Tesla always ate as though he were at a formal dinner, with each cup and plate in its place. He had been afraid of germs since he was a boy, and he used stacks of napkins—preferably 18, a number divisible by 3, another one of his obsessions—with each meal to clean his hands and silverware. And although he often stayed up all night working on an experiment, he always tried to be alert the next day.

Tesla wasn't the only inventor staying up all night. Before the discoveries of the late 1800s, people still depended on oil lamps and steam engines. Dozens of inventors throughout the world were racing to be the first to create a dependable light bulb, send power from one city to another, and transmit messages without wires. It was a tangled and disorderly process, with each inventor building on the discoveries of others.

Nikola Tesla raced with the others, but he was usually one step ahead of them. Born at midnight between 9 and 10 July 1856 in Smiljan, Croatia, Tesla was, from his boyhood, able to solve complicated problems in his head. He called his mind his mental blackboard and he would use it to work out the details of an invention and then put it to use in real life. Tesla even boasted of his early forays into inventing, "I needed no models, drawings, or experiments. I could picture them all as real in my mind."

Tesla had a good model for his creative mind. His mother invented kitchen tools and was famous for the fine needlework and weaving she did on a loom she designed herself. Tesla followed her example for original thinking. When he was very young, he caught frogs with a fishing rod he designed and built, complete with hook and line. He also built a motor powered by June bugs and experimented with a flying machine. When he saw a picture of Niagara Falls, he imagined a big wheel run by water like the ones he built in the creek near his home. The challenge to create a waterwheel that would harness and generate the awesome force of water flowing over Niagara Falls stayed with Tesla until he was an adult.

---

forays: attempts
harness: to rein in; to collect
generate: to bring about or produce

And Tesla could never pass up a challenge. When he was at college in Austria, he saw that the DC (direct current) electric motors people used then were inefficient and noisy. These motors sparked and rattled because they used a moving part called a commutator to convert electricity from the wires into the motion of a spinning shaft. Tesla told his professor that he could invent an AC (alternating current) motor that would work without a commutator, and the professor laughed at him, calling it "an impossible idea. Mr. Tesla may accomplish great things," the professor said, "but he will never do this."

But Tesla believed it could be done, and though he went on to other projects, he kept thinking about the AC motor. Just as he did when he was a boy, Tesla built the experiments in his mind instead of on a workbench. But one day in 1882 while he was walking in a park with a friend, the answer came to him as, he said, "a flash of lightning, and in an instant the truth was revealed."

On his mental blackboard, Tesla saw the spinning shaft of a motor powered by two out-of-step alternating currents, with no need for a commutator. Other inventors had solved parts of the problem, but no one had visualized a complete AC motor. Tesla was so excited that he grabbed a stick and drew a diagram in the dirt to explain the machine to his friend.

All generators make electricity by spinning the positive and negative poles of a magnet past a coiled wire, and the current they produce is alternating—that is, it jumps back and forth between positive and negative many times a second. Early scientists believed that such a current was useless, so they designed motors that changed it. These first motors used commutators that moved back and forth between the magnetic poles. Commutators switched the current so that it flowed only in one direction, thereby creating direct current. But commutators sparked and clattered as they worked.

---

inefficient: wasteful of energy or resources
commutator: a series of metal bars that, as part of an electrical generator, produce direct current
shaft: a pole

Tesla's diagram—and his invention—took the alternating current from two different wires instead of just one. By timing the currents in the wires so they were out of step with each other, he used them to spin the shaft the way two legs pedaling a bicycle can spin the wheels. This eliminated the commutator and made the motors run more quietly and safely. Tesla patented the first of his AC motors in 1890, and today nearly all electric motors are based on his invention.

When he was still a young man, Tesla went to the United States to work for Thomas Edison in his New Jersey laboratory. By that time, 1884, Edison was already famous for a number of inventions, including the incandescent light bulb.

Edison immediately gave Tesla the job of repairing the DC generators used to power a large ship. Tesla not only did the job overnight, but he also told Edison that he could redesign the generators so that they would work better and save money. Edison was impressed by Tesla's work, but when Tesla tried to convince him that AC generators would work better than DC, Edison got angry, saying, "Spare me that nonsense. We're set up for direct current in America."

Edison was the opposite of Tesla in almost every way, and they soon came to dislike each other. While Tesla was neat and dignified, Edison often slept in his lab for days at a time, and his clothes were rumpled and dirty. Edison had a large home and family, while Tesla believed such things would distract him, and he never married. Tesla cared little for the business side of inventing, but Edison was a shrewd bargainer when it came to contracts and payments. Tesla was proud of his university degree while Edison was entirely self-educated. His method of invention was trial and error, which Tesla considered slow and inefficient. "If Edison had a needle to find in a haystack," Tesla said, "he would proceed at once with the diligence of the bee to examine straw after straw until he found the object of his search."

incandescent: glowing as a result of intense heat
diligence: careful attention

With all these differences, it was difficult for the two inventors to get along, and after a disagreement about payment for his work, Tesla walked out. The biggest dispute they had, however, was over electric power itself. Edison's bulbs operated on DC power, while Tesla believed that AC was the way of the future. Edison already operated the Edison Electric Company, which generated DC power for a small number of houses and factories in New York City, and Tesla soon opened the Tesla Electric Company to develop an AC power system. When investors chose sides and tried to convince the public that their way was better, a "battle of the currents" began.

Today we know that AC power is better for large users like cities while DC works best in batteries. Tesla was correct when he pointed out that DC could only be transmitted a few miles before the lights grew dim. AC could travel over hundreds of miles of wire and still light a home. In the end the facts won out, and AC power runs our cities and industries today.

Like most inventors, Tesla often solved parts of a problem, and others took his work further. While still at Edison's lab, he worked on an idea for creating light through a gas instead of a filament, and that idea became the fluorescent lights we use today. Tesla was able to send wireless transmissions—soon to be known as radio—in 1893, and the inventor Guglielmo Marconi later used his ideas to build a device that sent a radio signal across the Atlantic Ocean.

Although Tesla was one of the most famous people in the world at the turn of the century, and though he received many honors for his work, his name was often left out of early books and articles by scientists, usually because Tesla was careless about applying for patents and signing contracts with the manufacturers of his inventions. He had little patience with those who thought only of money.

But some of Tesla's ideas seemed so bizarre that people decided they shouldn't believe in his work. He built a laboratory in Colorado where he tried to generate one hundred million volts of electricity in order to use what he called the earth's "resonant frequency" to send signals around the world without wires.

---

dispute: an argument
filament: a small wire that glows when an electrical current passes through it

He even said that if the inhabitants of Mars knew how to receive his signals, he could talk to them, too. At one point, he sent lightning bolts 135 feet in the air, and the nearby city of Colorado Springs went dark when he shorted out their power system.

Tesla could also be arrogant and impatient with people he worked with, and some newspaper reporters called him crazy and unreliable. But there was a little truth in even his most outrageous ideas, and his peculiar personality was the flip side of his genius. Tesla laughed at his critics.

"The present is theirs," Tesla said. "The future, for which I really worked, is mine."

Today Tesla's achievements speak for themselves. AC power, the system the world runs on today, uses motors and generators based on Tesla's inventions. If you visit Niagara Falls, you will see that he fulfilled his childhood dream of the waterwheel. His name appears nine times on the dedication plaque there, for nine separate inventions used in his great AC dynamos. The tesla, a unit of magnetic induction, is named for him. And every TV and radio uses a device called a Tesla coil that boosts the household current. This same device is also used for Hollywood special effects, like the blue lightning arching up the buzzing metal coil in Frankenstein movies. His work with electricity and magnetism formed some of the building blocks for lasers, radar, fax machines, and electron microscopes.

---

arrogant: conceited, full of oneself

HEALING A WOUNDED HEART:
DANIEL HALE WILLIAMS

William Orem

Chicago, 1893, a quiet summer evening—a man, his face clenched in agony, his shirt stained with blood, stumbles through the doors of Provident Hospital.

Fortunately for the wounded man, who was black, this hospital gave care to patients of any color—which was more than could be said of many of the hospitals in the city, indeed, in the whole United States.

Provident Hospital had been founded in 1891 by Dr. Daniel Hale Williams. Williams himself had come a long way before founding the hospital. He was born in Pennsylvania in 1856, before the Civil War, at a time when almost four million African Americans in the United States were still slaves. Daniel's parents, however, were not slaves. His father owned a barbershop. As a boy, Daniel started to learn the shoemaking trade. Later, he worked in barbershops as well. All the while, he studied hard and read constantly in order to learn all that he could.

As a young man, Daniel Hale Williams worked as an apprentice to a well-respected surgeon, Dr. Henry Palmer. This apprenticeship prepared Williams to enter Chicago Medical School, one of the best medical schools in the nation at the time. After three years of hard work, Williams graduated with his M.D. degree in 1883.

When Dr. Williams set up his medical practice, there were only three other black doctors in Chicago. He worked at the South Side Dispensary, where he was often called upon to make use of

---

clenched: held tightly
M.D.: *Medicinae Doctor* (Latin) = Doctor of Medicine
dispensary: a place where medicine or medical treatment is given out

his skills in surgery. He also provided medical care for children at a nearby orphanage and taught anatomy at the medical college where he had studied.

Wherever he looked, Dr. Williams saw few opportunities for African Americans to enter medical professions. He also saw that black people were sometimes refused medical care, or did not receive the same quality of care available to white people. That is why, when the Reverend Louis Reynolds came to him with an idea, Dr. Williams saw the wisdom of it. They would start their own hospital—a place where black people could get the same quality treatment as white people. The hospital would also serve as a training school for nurses—a goal dear to the heart of Reverend Reynolds, whose sister wanted to become a nurse but had been rejected from existing schools simply because she was black.

With support from other clergymen, wealthy donors, and community residents, Provident Hospital opened its doors in May of 1891. It gave patients equal access to quality care, and doctors and nurses equal access to quality training. In fact, Provident was the first hospital in the United States in which black and white doctors worked together to care for all patients, regardless of race.

On the summer night that the man with the knife wound stumbled into Provident Hospital, Dr. Williams was called in. The doctor reassured the patient with his calm, dignified manner. Williams was confident that he could help. But then he saw the wound—it went deep into the chest, perhaps into the heart.

At this time, the X-ray machine had not been invented, so there was no way for Dr. Williams to look inside the patient to determine the extent of the injury. No way, that is, except to open the man's chest and look right into it.

Open the chest? In 1893, doctors operated on torn muscles, on broken bones, even on serious knife wounds to other parts of the body. But they did not perform heart surgery. Many doctors argued that it was too dangerous; they said a surgeon would be foolish even to try such a thing.

---

anatomy: the scientific study of the parts and structures of living things

Yes, it was dangerous. But Daniel Hale Williams was not foolish—on the contrary, he was very careful. He knew that, unless he took this risk, the patient was almost sure to die.

With several other doctors observing and assisting, Dr. Williams started the operation. He cut into the man's chest. He cut even deeper. He examined the depth of the stab wound. He found and repaired a torn blood vessel. He stitched up the pericardium, a fluid-filled bag that surrounds the heart. He very carefully cleaned the wound and the chest cavity, to make sure that no infection set in. Then he stitched closed the man's chest, again taking great care to keep everything as antiseptic as he could.

The surgery was a success. The wounded man lived, not only for the rest of that day, or the rest of that week, but for decades afterward. Dr. Williams had given him back his life. In the process, he became the first doctor to perform successful heart surgery.

Dr. Williams wasn't trying to become a hero on that evening in 1893, nor could he have known he was going to become famous for his accomplishment. But the newspapers let the world know, in dramatic headlines that read, "Sewed Up His Heart!"

Dr. Williams went on to become chief surgeon at the Freedman's Hospital in Washington, D.C. He reorganized the hospital and made it into a model of high quality medical care.

Daniel Hale Williams was successful in many ways. He worked hard to become a doctor at a time when the doors of the medical profession were generally closed to African Americans. He remained committed to his belief that all people deserve quality health care. And as a surgeon, he was bold enough to take risks but careful enough to ensure the safety of his patients.

antiseptic: free of germs
ensure: to guarantee or make sure

Marie Curie and the Discovery of Radioactivity

Mara Rockliff

"Marie! It's here!" shouted Pierre. "Our shipment has arrived!"

Marie Curie did not even pause to grab her hat. She rushed out into the street after her husband. There it was—a big, heavy wagon, like the ones that brought much-needed coal for their lab's dilapidated stove. But this wagon carried a far more precious and exciting load.

A moment later, people passing by the School of Physics and Chemistry were treated to a sight not often seen on the fashionable streets of Paris in the early 1900s: a bareheaded young woman in a laboratory smock, ripping eagerly into the pile of heavy sacks and burying her hands in... *dirt?*

To the Austrian mine owners who had sent the pitchblende ore, it was just dirt. After all, they had already taken out the valuable part—the metallic element called uranium—and dumped what was left over in a nearby pine forest. If a pair of eccentric French scientists wanted them to scoop up the worthless stuff and ship it, the mine owners were happy to oblige.

But Marie and Pierre Curie knew the secret of the dull brown ore. Hidden deep within it was a new chemical element. No one, the Curies included, had ever seen this element. Still, the husband-and-wife team had given it a name: radium. And Marie was determined to prove radium was real.

---

dilapidated: run-down; neglected and in poor condition
physics: a branch of science concerned with the relationship between matter
    and energy
pitchblende: a brownish-black mineral that is uncommonly high in
    radioactive elements
ore: rock or mineral from which a valuable element may be extracted
eccentric: odd; unusual in one's behavior
oblige: to help

No one knew how difficult the task would be. But Marie, although still a student, had already shown that she possessed the most important quality of a successful scientist. When it came to the search for knowledge, she never gave up.

When she was growing up in Russian-occupied Poland, even to study science was forbidden. Many nights, young Maria Sklodowska (as she was then named) slipped through the dark streets of Warsaw on her way to an illegal night school, glancing anxiously over her shoulder for any sign of the Russian police. Days, she worked teaching children, saving her rubles to send her older sister to medical school in the city of intellectual freedom—Paris, France.

At last, her own turn came. Her sister, newly married, sent for Marie to join her in Paris. Clutching a blanket and a folding chair—the fourth-class train ticket, all she could afford, did not provide even a seat—she hugged the rest of her family goodbye. When Marie arrived in Paris in 1891, she studied physics at the greatest university in Europe, the Sorbonne. But how poor she was! And how poorly prepared! She barely knew enough French, let alone advanced math and science, to understand the lectures.

Marie studied late into the evenings in the library, struggling to catch up with her classmates. Then she climbed the six flights to her little room. In the winter, it was so cold that she emptied her closet, piling the clothes on her bed so she'd be warm enough to sleep. Sometimes she had no money to buy even an egg or a loaf of bread. But then, how could she take the time to stop studying long enough to cook?

Her hard work was rewarded. Marie won her degree in physics, graduating first in her class. And the next year she earned a second degree, in mathematics. She also met the man who soon became her husband—Pierre Curie, a brilliant young physicist as promising (and as poor) as Marie. Their love for each other was equaled only by their shared love of science.

It was a thrilling time to be a scientist. The year the Curies were married, 1895, a German physicist named Wilhelm Roentgen discovered a new kind of ray that could be used to "see" inside people and photograph their bones. He called them X rays. The X stood for "unknown."

Not long after, the French physicist Henri Becquerel discovered that uranium let out another type of ray. These rays were weak compared to X rays, and even Becquerel himself did not think his discovery of much importance. But Marie found the rays fascinating. Where did they come from? How were they produced? She decided to examine these mysterious "Becquerel rays" for her advanced research.

She set to work. Day after day, Marie experimented with uranium under all kinds of conditions: dry and wet; powdered and solid; pure and mixed with other elements. She heated the uranium, and shone lights on it. Then, using a special instrument called an electrometer, which Pierre and his brother had invented, she measured the uranium rays and carefully copied the numbers down in her notebook.

The results were astonishing. It didn't seem to matter what she did to the uranium. Nothing affected the strength of the rays—nothing but the amount of uranium present. The energy appeared to come from inside the metal itself, deep down at the level of its atoms. Marie named this atomic energy *radioactivity.* A substance that emitted this energy was called *radioactive.*

Her experiments yielded a second surprise. A sample of uranium-rich pitchblende turned out to be three or four times as radioactive as pure uranium. How could this be? Marie had already tested every known element in pitchblende. None was radioactive. But something in that pitchblende, something besides the uranium, was sending out rays.

There could only be one answer. If the extra radioactivity could not be coming from any known element, it must be coming from an *unknown* element.

Pierre was so excited by Marie's discovery that he dropped his own research on crystals to assist her. They knew the new element, which they decided to call radium, must be extremely tiny to have escaped notice all these years. Maybe it made up as little of the pitchblende as one percent! And yet this tiny bit of radium gave off stronger rays than a much larger amount of uranium. It must be powerfully radioactive.

The mine owners had sent them seven tons of pitchblende. Somewhere in that seven tons, Pierre and Marie were convinced, they would find radium.

It was like searching for a needle in a very large haystack—except that they had no way of knowing what this "needle" even looked like. And the needle would turn out to be much smaller than either of them imagined. It was not one percent. It was less than one *millionth* of one percent.

No one paid the Curies to do this work. They could not even persuade the School of Physics, where Pierre taught, to let them use a laboratory. Instead, they were forced to set up shop in an abandoned shed.

A visitor once described the Curies' laboratory as "a cross between a stable and a potato cellar." In summer, the heat was stifling. In winter, the old stove barely gave out enough warmth to thaw their frozen hands. The roof leaked when it rained.

"Yet," Marie would write years later, "it was in this miserable old shed that we passed the best and happiest years of our life, devoting our entire days to our work."

The work could be backbreaking. Marie spent many hours boiling down pitchblende in enormous pots, stirring the heavy mixture with an iron rod as tall as she was, gasping and coughing from the fumes. Later, she faced the nearly impossible task of producing purer and purer samples in the drafty, dusty shed with its dirt floor.

A year, two years, three years. Marie edged closer to her goal. Sometimes, in the evenings, she and Pierre put their little daughter to bed, leaving her in the care of her grandfather. Then the couple would walk arm in arm through the Paris streets, returning to their darkened laboratory to gaze at the old wooden tables full of tubes and bottles glowing with a faint blue light.

Finally, one day in 1902, they were able to make their announcement to the world. Marie and Pierre Curie had a pure sample of a new element called radium, thousands of times more radioactive than uranium. And it was useful. While Marie had labored to purify radium, Pierre had been experimenting with her samples. He discovered that radium could kill cancer cells. Compared to surgery or to chemicals used to treat cancer at the time, radium was much safer and more effective.

stifling: extremely stuffy, hot, and uncomfortable

Radium rapidly became big business. A single gram was worth $100,000. Manufacturers made their fortunes making and selling radium, using the methods Marie had developed. But Marie and Pierre refused to charge a penny for their discovery. They believed that the true spirit of science meant sharing knowledge freely.

The discovery of radioactivity would turn out to be useful in many ways. For example, among other things, doctors now use radioactive dyes to help diagnose medical problems, and scientists can use radioactivity to determine the age of fossils.

In 1903 Marie became Doctor Marie Curie. The professors who judged her work—outstanding scientists themselves—told her that no advanced research had ever made such a great contribution to science.

Later that same year, she earned an even higher honor for her research. Along with Henri Becquerel, the Curies were awarded the Nobel Prize for physics. Marie Curie became the first woman ever to win a Nobel Prize.

She would go on to win a second Nobel Prize, in chemistry, making her the first person ever to be awarded the Nobel Prize twice. And the Sorbonne made her its first female professor. But all these "firsts" meant little to Marie Curie. For her, what came first was always science.

ENRICO FERMI: THE "ITALIAN NAVIGATOR"

Dorothy Haas

On a gray December day in 1942, a strange telephone call was made between Chicago and Cambridge, Massachusetts. Dr. Arthur Compton, director of the Manhattan Project, was calling Dr. James B. Conant, chairman of the National Defense Research Committee. Because the United States was at war, they spoke in a kind of code. Nobody listening in could have understood them. But Dr. Conant knew of secret experiments being carried out in Chicago. He understood.

"I have just left the Italian navigator," said Dr. Compton. "He has arrived safely on the shores of the new world."

There was a tension-packed pause at the other end of the wire. "Oh?" said Dr. Conant after a minute. "And how did he find the natives?"

"Friendly!" said Dr. Compton happily. "Most friendly!"

A scholarly-looking man hurried down Ellis Avenue on Chicago's south side. An icy wind whipped winter's first snowflakes about him. But he stepped out briskly, breathing deeply of the cold air. Dr. Enrico Fermi—physicist, university professor, Nobel Prize winner—enjoyed the outdoors.

He turned in at a big stone entrance built like an old castle. It was the west gate of Stagg Field, the University of Chicago's unused football stadium. Inside, he made his way to a building that sat huddled beneath the deserted west stands.

Once the building had been a squash court. It had echoed with the *squash!* sound of a little black ball and the excited calls of the boys who played there. But the building was a squash court no longer. Now it was called the "Metallurgical Laboratory." The scientists who worked there were sworn to absolute secrecy.

---

metallurgical: having to do with metals and their properties

Their mysterious experiments had nothing at all to do with the science of metals. The squash-court laboratory had become a top secret division of a United States Government agency called the Manhattan Project.

The scientist paused in the hallway of the building. He slipped out of his overcoat and shrugged into a lab coat that was streaked with black. Then he turned toward the lab. A young man was just coming out. He too wore a grimy lab coat. And he had been handling something black, as the smudges on his cheek gave proof. Whatever the experiments going on in the little building, one thing was certain—they were dirty!

Seeing his chief, the young man stopped. "Morning, Doctor," he said. He nodded down at a bottle he carried. "They're mixing the cadmium solution over at the lab right now. It'll be ready when you need it."

"And the checklist?" asked Dr. Fermi.

"That's ready too," the young man said. "It's with your things up in the gallery."

He moved on. Dr. Fermi went on into his laboratory—into a forbidding, dusky scene.

The walls of the room were black. The floor was black. At one end of the room, surrounded by a boxlike wooden framework, was a big black ball, flattened on top. The ball was made of graphite, the material commonly found in lead pencils. It was dust from the graphite ball that had turned everything in the laboratory an eerie black.

But never mind the dust! That graphite ball—the scientists called it a "pile"—was going to do something that few men believed possible. It was going to split the atom!

Atoms might be called the building blocks of all matter. The chairs we sit in, the food we eat, the water we drink, the air we breathe, the clothes we wear—all are made up of atoms. But atoms cannot be seen. They are almost the tiniest particles imaginable.

---

cadmium: a bluish-white metallic element
gallery: a room or balcony from which people watch an event

Imagine that you have an iron ball, one that can be cut in half as easily as an apple. Then suppose you cut one of these two pieces in half. Imagine that you keep on dividing the ball in this way, always taking one piece and cutting it in half. At last nothing would remain but a single, tiny invisible speck of iron—an atom. Imagine that you can see this atom.

You would find it made up of several parts, all of them constantly moving. The parts are called protons, neutrons, and electrons. The protons and neutrons form the core, the nucleus, of the atom. The electrons spin around the nucleus at an amazing speed. The parts of the atom are held together by an enormous strength. Try as you might, you couldn't cut the last atom of the iron ball in half.

Scientists had known of atoms and this hidden strength for many years. They had often talked about how wonderful it would be if the tremendous energy holding the atom together could be set free for man's use. But they had always thought that it would take more energy to split the atom than could be obtained from the division. Then, late in the nineteen thirties, certain discoveries were made, discoveries that shed light on the inner workings of the atom.

One man in particular thought the atom could be split to obtain unheard-of amounts of energy. He was Dr. Enrico Fermi, an Italian physicist. Dr. Fermi had come to live in the United States when he found that he was no longer able to live under a fascist form of government.

Dr. Fermi had done much work on the neutron. This work had won the Nobel Prize for him. It was work that led directly to the building of the first atomic pile at the University of Chicago.

Neutrons, said Dr. Fermi, could be made to shoot into the cores of atoms, splitting them apart. Furthermore, he said that once the process started, the neutrons set free would act upon other atoms, releasing still more energy and even more neutrons. He called this process "self-sustaining chain reaction."

---

fascist: relating to a kind of government that denies freedom and is usually run by a dictator

The scientist faced many problems in trying to split the atom. But one problem stood out above all the others. Neutrons moved with lightning speed. A way had to be found to slow them down in their headlong flight. Otherwise they would fly off and be lost before they did their atom-splitting work.

The scientists tested many materials that they hoped might slow down the neutrons. At last Dr. Fermi thought he had the answer.

"Pure graphite should slow down the neutrons," he said. "Let us make a pile of graphite and uranium. When we have built it to just the right size, more neutrons will be trapped within the pile than can escape from it. When that happens, neutrons will begin splitting the uranium atoms and will continue to do so in a chain reaction."

Materials were hard to find. Ordinary graphite was plentiful enough. But absolutely pure graphite had to be made. And that took time. Furthermore, uranium was very scarce.

Materials arrived slowly at the laboratory. But arrive they did. At last, in the spring of 1942, the scientists were able to begin. They piled up the graphite and uranium around a source of free neutrons that would set off the pile. Then they tested it with sensitive instruments.

Yes, Dr. Fermi decided, they seemed to be on the right track. But their pile had to be bigger; too many neutrons were still escaping from it. They took down the small pile. In the fall of 1942 they began another, a bigger, one.

The materials were placed in layers. First a layer of graphite bricks was put down. This was followed by a layer of bricks that had pieces of uranium sealed in their hollowed-out cores. Slowly that pile took shape.

At last the day came when the pile was ready to be tested. It was December 2, 1942.

Dr. Fermi walked around the pile, looking at it. The big black ball nearly touched the ceiling. He slid his hand along one of the control rods.

"In these slim rods," he thought, "lies the safety of all the people in this laboratory!"

---

uranium: a radioactive metallic element

The control rods were made of cadmium. They were thrust deep into the center of the pile. There they soaked up neutrons in much the same way sponges soak up water. When they were pulled out of the pile, the neutrons would be free to split the uranium atoms. If anything went wrong, if the pile began reacting too fast, the control rods would fall back into place. They would stop the action of the pile.

Further, a group of three young men would be seated on a platform above the pile with jugs of cadmium solution. If danger threatened, they would break the jugs. The solution would pour down into the pile. It would help the control rods soak up the neutrons.

But nothing should go wrong! Mathematics had told the scientists just how to build the pile. Mathematics had told them what would happen inside of it.

And yet... The scientists were like men who know all about flying from having studied about it in books, but who have never actually flown a plane. As atom-splitters, the scientists knew all about it from their figures, but they had never actually split an atom. The control rods were like automatic pilots, ready to take over in case of trouble.

Fermi turned to a young scientist working nearby. "Is everything ready here on the floor?" he asked.

"Ready as it'll ever be," the young man answered. "All of the rods except one will come out before we begin. I'll handle the last one myself. You just give the orders."

Satisfied that everything was running smoothly on the main floor, Dr. Fermi went up to his gallery. His instruments were placed there. They would tell him, minute by minute, what was going on inside the pile. With these instruments, he would chart a safe, steady course for the reaction that would take place inside the big pile.

The morning hours slipped away. The instruments were checked and rechecked. Everyone in the laboratory had a job. Everyone went about his work quietly and surely.

At last Dr. Fermi looked at his watch. The test could begin. All the scientists who had worked on the project crowded into the gallery. There was excited chatter.

"Keep your eye on the counters!"

"…what this will mean if…"

"…what people in the neighborhood would think if they…"

Gradually a hush settled over the group. All eyes turned to Dr. Fermi. He did not show excitement. He was calm.

"We will withdraw the last cadmium rod inches at a time," he said. "Each time we will check our instruments."

"Ready down there?" he called to the main floor.

"Ready," came the cool reply.

"Now!" commanded Dr. Fermi.

The watchers grew tense. The young scientist pulled the rod a little way out of the pile.

At once the instruments in the gallery showed what was happening inside the pile. The steady *click click click* of the counters began to sound faster. Lights flashed on the panels. The first few neutrons were shooting into uranium atoms!

Dr. Fermi watched his instruments carefully. He noted the changes they showed. He was like a ship's captain moving through dangerous, shallow waters. A ship's captain takes soundings, tests, before he moves ahead. Dr. Fermi was taking his own kind of soundings; only when the nervous clicking of the counters leveled off into a steady rhythm, showing that the way ahead was safe, did he give the order to move forward.

"All right," he said. "Pull out more of the rod."

Once again the watchers tensed. And once again they relaxed. Nothing more than a quickening of the instruments showed what was happening below.

Morning wore into afternoon. Little by little the long rod was pulled from the center of the pile. Little by little activity inside the pile increased, then leveled off. A full reaction could not take place as long as any part of the rod remained in the pile.

At last, at 3:25, the final order was given.

"The rest of the rod can now come out of the pile," said Dr. Fermi.

There was no sound in the laboratory—not from the men who watched, nor from the big pile itself. But the instruments told their story. The lights flashed the message for all to see. The counters clicked excitedly for all to hear.

Inside the black ball neutrons that had no means of escape were slamming into uranium atoms. They were splitting those atoms, releasing a new kind of energy, greater than any man had ever known.

Dr. Fermi was silent. He studied his instruments for a long time.

"You can replace the rod now," he called then, and turned to the scientists who had helped to build the pile.

"The pile created a half watt of power," he said. "The amount is really quite unimportant, as you must realize, since we can increase it at will."

He looked around him, smiling quietly. "What is really important," he said, "is that we have established something new here today—a self-sustaining chain reaction!"

Hubbub broke out in the gallery. Amid congratulations and the slapping of backs, Enrico Fermi's mind was far away. "Science has opened the doors to a wonderful new world today," he thought. "Who knows what awaits us there!"

---

hubbub: great noise and confusion

Advice and Instruction

The Fish I Didn't Catch

John Greenleaf Whittier

Our bachelor uncle who lived with us was a quiet, genial man, much given to hunting and fishing; and it was one of the pleasures of our young life to accompany him on his expeditions to Great Hill, Brandy-brow Woods, the Pond, and, best of all, to the Country Brook. We were quite willing to work hard in the cornfield or the haying lot to finish the necessary day's labor in season for an afternoon stroll through the woods and along the brookside.

I remember my first fishing excursion as if it were but yesterday. I have been happy many times in my life, but never more intensely so than when I received that first fishing pole from my uncle's hand, and trudged off with him through the woods and meadows. It was a still, sweet day of early summer; the long afternoon shadows of the trees lay cool across our path; the leaves seemed greener, the flowers brighter, the birds merrier, than ever before.

My uncle, who knew by long experience where were the best haunts of pickerel, considerately placed me at the most favorable point. I threw out my line as I had so often seen others, and waited anxiously for a bite, moving the bait in rapid jerks on the surface of the water in imitation of the leap of a frog. Nothing came of it. "Try again," said my uncle. Suddenly the bait sank out of sight. "Now for it," thought I; "here is a fish at last."

---

genial: friendly; kind
excursion: a trip
trudged: walked (usually with effort)
haunts: places often visited
pickerel: a small, freshwater fish

I made a strong pull, and brought up a tangle of weeds. Again and again I cast out my line with aching arms, and drew it back empty. I looked at my uncle appealingly. "Try once more," he said; "we fishermen must have patience."

Suddenly something tugged at my line, and swept off with it into deep water. Jerking it up, I saw a fine pickerel wriggling in the sun. "Uncle!" I cried, looking back in uncontrollable excitement, "I've got a fish!"

"Not yet," said my uncle. As he spoke there was splash in the water; I caught the arrowy gleam of a scared fish shooting into the middle of the stream—my hook hung empty from the line. I had lost my prize.

We are apt to speak of the sorrows of childhood as trifles in comparison with those of grown-up people; but we may depend upon it the young folks don't agree with us. Our griefs, modified and restrained by reason, experience, and self-respect, keep the proprieties, and, if possible, avoid a scene; but the sorrow of childhood, unreasoning and all-absorbing, is a complete abandonment to the passion. The doll's nose is broken, and the world breaks up with it; the marble rolls out of sight, and the solid globe rolls off with the marble.

So, overcome with my great and bitter disappointment, I sat down on the nearest hassock, and for a time refused to be comforted, even by my uncle's assurance that there were more fish in the brook. He refitted my bait, and, putting the pole again in my hands, told me to try my luck once more.

"But remember, boy," he said, with his shrewd smile, "never brag of catching a fish until he is on dry ground. I've seen older folks doing that in more ways than one, and so making fools of themselves. It's no use to boast of anything until it's done, nor then, either, for it speaks for itself."

---

arrowy: like an arrow
apt: likely
trifles: unimportant things
hassock: a tussock, that is, a thick clump of grass

How often since I have been reminded of the fish that I did not catch. When I hear people boasting of a work as yet undone, and trying to anticipate the credit which belongs only to actual achievement, I call to mind that scene by the brookside, and the wise caution of my uncle in that particular instance takes the form of a proverb of universal application: "Never brag of your fish before you catch him."

---

anticipate: to expect; to look forward to something as certain though it is yet to happen

proverb: a short, well-known saying containing a wise thought

WORK

John Ruskin

It is physically impossible for a well-educated, intellectual, or brave man to make money the chief object of his thoughts—as physically impossible as it is for him to make his dinner the principal object of them. All healthy people like their dinners, but their dinner is not the main object of their lives. So all healthily minded people like making money—ought to like it, and to enjoy the sensation of winning it; but the main object of their life is not money; it is something better than money.

A good soldier, for instance, mainly wishes to do his fighting well. He is glad of his pay—very properly so, and justly grumbles when you keep him ten years without it; still, his main notion of life is to win battles, not to be paid for winning them.

So of doctors. They like fees no doubt—ought to like them; yet if they are brave and well educated, the entire object of their lives is not fees. They, on the whole, desire to cure the sick; and—if they are good doctors, and the choice were fairly put to them—would rather cure their patient and lose their fee than kill him and get it. And so with all other brave and rightly trained men; their work is first, their fee second; very important always, but still second.

But in every nation, as I said, there are a vast class who are cowardly, and more or less stupid. And with these people, just as certainly the fee is first and the work second, as with brave people the work is first and the fee *second*.

And this is no small distinction. It is the whole distinction in a man. You cannot serve two masters; you *must* serve one or the other. If your work is first with you, and your fee second, work is your master.

---

object: purpose; goal
winning it [money]: gaining or earning money

Observe then, all wise work is mainly threefold in character. It is honest, useful, and cheerful. I hardly know anything more strange than that you recognize honesty in play, and you do not in work. In your lightest games you have always some one to see what you call "fair play." In boxing, you must hit fair; in racing, start fair. Your watchword is fair play; your hatred, foul play. Did it ever strike you that you wanted another watchword also, fair work, and another hatred also, foul work?

threefold: having three parts
watchword: motto; guiding principle

Honest Work

Men said the old smith was foolishly careful, as he wrought on the great chain he was making in his dingy shop in the heart of the great city. But he heeded not their words, and only wrought with greater painstaking. Link after link he fashioned and welded and finished, and at last the great chain was completed.

Years passed. One night there was a terrible storm, and a ship was in sore peril of being dashed upon the rocks. Anchor after anchor was dropped, but none of them held. The cables were broken like threads.

At last the mighty sheet anchor was cast into the sea, and the old chain quickly uncoiled and ran out till it grew taut. All watched to see if it would bear the awful strain. It sang in the wild storm as the vessel's weight surged upon it. It was a moment of intense anxiety. The ship with its cargo of a thousand lives depended upon this one chain. What now if the old smith had wrought carelessly even one link of his chain!

But he had put honesty and truth and invincible strength into every part of it; and it stood the test, holding the ship in safety until the storm was over.

---

smith: blacksmith; one who forges iron
wrought: worked; shaped by hammering, cutting, and stretching
heeded not: paid no attention to
painstaking: careful work with great attention to detail
fashioned: shaped; formed
in sore peril: in extreme danger
sheet anchor: a large, strong anchor used only in emergencies
taut: tight; without any slack
invincible: unconquerable; incapable of being defeated

For Want of a Horseshoe Nail

adapted from James Baldwin

This is a legend about a real king, King Richard III of England, who is generally regarded as one of England's worst rulers. In 1485, Richard was defeated in a battle against troops led by Henry, Earl of Richmond. Many people remember the battle best because of a line written by William Shakespeare in his play, Richard III, *in which Richard cries out, "A horse! A horse! My kingdom for a horse!" Read on to understand the meaning of that desperate cry.*

The blacksmith paused from hammering the hot iron to wipe his sweaty brow.

"Hurry up, man, hurry up!" cried a man at his side. "You must shoe this horse quickly, for the king wishes to ride him into battle!"

"Indeed, sir," said the blacksmith, "so you think there will be a battle today?"

"Most certainly, and very soon, too," answered the man, with an air of importance. "Why, when I left the field, the king's enemies were on the march and ready for the fight. Today will decide whether Richard or Henry shall rule England. And as I am the king's groom, I charge you, sir, make haste, for the king prefers this steed to all others!"

"As you say, sir," muttered the blacksmith as he bent back to his tools, "though good work cannot be rushed."

From a bar of iron he made four horseshoes. Then he hammered and shaped and fitted them to the horse's feet. Then he began to nail them on. But after he had nailed on two shoes, he found that he did not have enough nails for the other two.

"Begging your pardon, sir," he said to the impatient groom, "but as I've had to shoe so many horses these past few days, I now have only six nails left, and it will take a little time to hammer out the rest I need."

---

groom: one who looks after horses
charge: to command; to place a responsibility upon

"You say you have six nails?" asked the groom with a stamp of his foot. "And only two shoes left to put on? Then put three nails in each shoe. That will have to do. Come, man, be quick about it. I think I hear the trumpets even now!"

The blacksmith cast him a doubtful look but did as he was told. He quickly finished the shoeing, and the groom hurried to lead the horse to the king.

The battle had been raging for some time. King Richard rode up and down the field, urging his men and slashing at his foes. His enemy, Henry, was pressing him hard.

Far away at the other side of the field, King Richard saw his men falling back in confusion. "Press forward! Press forward!" he yelled. Then he spurred his horse to ride toward the broken line and rally the men to turn and fight.

He was hardly halfway across the stony field when one of the horse's shoes flew off. A few steps more and another shoe came off. The horse stumbled, and King Richard was thrown to the ground.

Before the king could rise, his frightened horse had galloped away. The king looked up and saw that his soldiers were fleeing in confused retreat, and that on all sides Henry's troops were closing in upon him.

He waved his sword in the air and shouted, "A horse! A horse! My kingdom for a horse!"

But there was no horse for him. His soldiers rushed past, intent on saving themselves.

The battle was lost. King Richard was lost. And Henry became king of England.

And since that time, people have said:

For want of a nail, the shoe was lost,
For want of a shoe, the horse was lost,
For want of a horse, the battle was lost,
For want of a battle, the kingdom was lost,
And all for the want of a horseshoe nail.

---

spurred: urged on and directed with spurs
rally: to rouse; to inspire toward a common purpose
intent: focused on some purpose

ARGUMENT

Joseph Addison

Avoid disputes as much as possible, in order to appear easy and well bred in conversation. You may assure yourself it requires more wit, as well as more good-humor, to improve rather than contradict the notions of another; but if you are at any time obliged to enter an argument, give your reasons with the utmost candor and modesty, two qualities which will scarcely ever fail to make an impression upon your hearers.

Besides, if you are not dogmatic, and if you do not show by your words or actions that you are self-conceited, all present will more heartily rejoice at your victory; nay, should you be worsted in argument, you may make your retreat with very good grace. You were never positive, and are now glad to be better informed.

In order to keep that good temper which is so difficult and yet so necessary to preserve, you should consider that nothing can be more unjust or ridiculous than to be angry with another because he is not of your opinion. The interests, education, and means by which men obtain their knowledge are so very different that it is impossible they should all think alike; and he has at least as much reason to be angry with you as you with him.

Sometimes, to keep yourself cool, it may be of service to ask yourself fairly what would be your opinion if you had all the biases of education or interest your adversary may have. But if you

---

well bred: brought up well; raised properly
wit: intelligence
contradict: to express an opposite opinion
utmost: of the greatest or highest degree
candor: honesty and openness
dogmatic: pushy and overbearing in stating an opinion
biases: preferences that shape judgment; prejudices
adversary: an opponent; a challenger

contend for the honor of victory alone, you may lay down this as an infallible maxim, that you cannot make a falser step, or give your antagonist a greater advantage over you, than to fall into a passion.

When an argument is over, how many weighty reasons does a man recollect which his heat and violence made him utterly forget?

It is still more absurd to be angry with a man because he does not apprehend the force of your reasons, or gives weak ones of his own. If you argue for reputation, this makes your victory the easier; he is certainly, in all respects, an object of your pity rather than of your anger; and if he cannot comprehend your reasoning, you ought to thank nature for having given you so much the clearer understanding.

You may please to add this consideration: that among your equals no one values your anger, which only preys upon its master; and, perhaps, you may find it not very consistent, either with prudence or with your ease, to punish yourself whenever you meet with a fool or a knave.

Lastly, if you propose to yourself the true end of argument, which is information, it may be a seasonable check to your passions; for if you search for truth only, it will be almost indifferent to you where you find it.

---

contend: to strive; to struggle for
infallible: perfect; always correct
maxim: a short piece of wisdom; a truism
antagonist: an enemy; an adversary
fall into a passion: to lose control of one's emotions; to display intense and
    uncontrolled emotion, especially anger
absurd: completely unreasonable; ridiculous
apprehend: to understand
preys upon: injures; makes a victim of
prudence: sound judgment; wisdom
knave: a tricky, dishonest person
seasonable: occurring in proper time
check: something that stops, holds back, or restrains
indifferent to: of no importance to; not mattering one way or another

If

Rudyard Kipling

If you can keep your head when all about you
    Are losing theirs and blaming it on you;
If you can trust yourself when all men doubt you,
    But make allowance for their doubting too;
If you can wait and not be tired by waiting,
    Or, being lied about, don't deal in lies,
Or, being hated, don't give way to hating,
    And yet don't look too good, nor talk too wise;

If you can dream—and not make dreams your master;
    If you can think—and not make thoughts your aim;
If you can meet with triumph and disaster
    And treat those two impostors just the same;
If you can bear to hear the truth you've spoken
    Twisted by knaves to make a trap for fools,
Or watch the things you gave your life to broken,
    And stoop and build 'em up with worn-out tools;

If you can make one heap of all your winnings
    And risk it on one turn of pitch-and-toss,
And lose, and start again at your beginnings
    And never breathe a word about your loss;
If you can force your heart and nerve and sinew
    To serve your turn long after they are gone,
And so hold on when there is nothing in you
    Except the Will which says to them: "Hold on!"

---

make allowance for: to grant the possibility of
impostors: deceivers; persons who try to trick by assuming a false identity
knaves: tricky, dishonest people
sinew: muscle

If you can talk with crowds and keep your virtue,
    Or walk with kings—nor lose the common touch;
If neither foes nor loving friends can hurt you;
    If all men count with you, but none too much;
If you can fill the unforgiving minute
    With sixty seconds' worth of distance run—
Yours is the Earth and everything that's in it,
    And—which is more—you'll be a Man, my son!

---

virtue: goodness; moral strength

CAN'T

Edgar Guest

Can't is the worst word that's written or spoken;
    Doing more harm here than slander and lies;
On it is many a strong spirit broken,
    And with it many a good purpose dies.
It springs from the lips of the thoughtless each morning
    And robs us of courage we need through the day:
It rings in our ears like a timely sent warning
    And laughs when we falter and fall by the way.

Can't is the father of feeble endeavor,
    The parent of terror and halfhearted work;
It weakens the efforts of artisans clever,
    And makes of the toiler an indolent shirk.
It poisons the soul of the man with a vision,
    It stifles in infancy many a plan;
It greets honest toiling with open derision
    And mocks at the hopes and the dreams of a man.

---

slander: false statements that damage a person's reputation
feeble: weak
endeavor: effort
artisans: artists and craftsmen
toiler: a worker
indolent: lazy
shirk: one who avoids work
stifles: smothers; holds back; suppresses
derision: ridicule; mockery
mocks at: ridicules; meanly makes fun of

Can't is a word none should speak without blushing;
  To utter it should be a symbol of shame;
Ambition and courage it daily is crushing;
  It blights a man's purpose and shortens his aim.
Despise it with all of your hatred of error;
  Refuse it the lodgment it seeks in your brain;
Arm against it as a creature of terror,
  And all that you dream of you someday shall gain.

Can't is the word that is foe to ambition
  An enemy ambushed to shatter your will;
Its prey is forever the man with a mission
  And bows but to courage and patience and skill.
Hate it, with hatred that's deep and undying,
  For once it is welcomed 'twill break any man;
Whatever the goal you are seeking, keep trying
  And answer this demon by saying: "I can."

---

ambition: strong desire to achieve
blights: ruins; destroys
lodgment: a place to stay
prey: hunted creature; victim
'twill: poetic shortened form of "it will"

LETTER TO HIS SON

Robert E. Lee

You must study to be frank with the world; frankness is the child of honesty and courage. Say just what you mean to do on every occasion and take it for granted you meant to do right. If a friend asks a favor, you should grant it if it is reasonable; if not, tell him plainly why you cannot; you will wrong him and wrong yourself by equivocation of any kind. Never do a wrong thing to make a friend or keep one; the man who requires you to do so is dearly purchased at a sacrifice. Deal kindly but firmly with all your classmates; you will find it the policy which wears best...

If you have any fault to find with anyone, tell him, not others, of what you complain; there is no more dangerous experiment than that of undertaking to be one thing before a man's face and another behind his back. We should live, act, and say nothing to the injury of anyone. It is not only best as a matter of principle but it is the path of peace and honor.

In regard to duty, let me, in conclusion of this hasty letter, inform you that nearly a hundred years ago there was a day of remarkable gloom and darkness—still known as "the dark day"— a day when the light of the sun was slowly extinguished as if by an eclipse. The Legislature of Connecticut was in session, and as the members saw the unexpected and unaccountable darkness coming on, they shared in the general awe and terror. It was supposed by many that the last day—the day of judgment—had come. Someone

---

study: to try hard
frank: candid; sincere
equivocation: misleading or deceptive language
dearly: at a very high price
policy: guiding principle; plan of action
hasty: hurried; quick
unaccountable: beyond any explanation; strange
awe: wonder; dread

in the consternation of the hour moved an adjournment. Then there arose an old Puritan legislator, Davenport of Stamford, and said that if the last day had come he desired to be found in his place doing his duty and therefore moved that candles be brought in, so that the House could proceed with its duty. There was quietness in that man's mind, the quietness of heavenly wisdom and inflexible willingness to obey present duty.

Duty, then, is the sublimest word in our language. Do your duty in all things, like the old Puritan. You cannot do more, you should never wish to do less. Never let me and your mother wear one gray hair for any lack of duty on your part.

---

consternation: state of confused amazement
adjournment: a break; the ending of an activity for a time
sublimest: greatest; most noble, admirable, and awe-inspiring

MOTHER TO SON

Langston Hughes

Well, son, I'll tell you:
Life for me ain't been no crystal stair.
It's had tacks in it,
And splinters,
And boards torn up,
And places with no carpet on the floor—
Bare.
But all the time
I'se been a-climbin' on,
And reachin' landin's,
And turnin' corners,
And sometimes goin' in the dark
Where there ain't been no light.
So boy, don't you turn back.
Don't you set down on the steps
'Cause you finds it's kinder hard.
Don't you fall now—
For I'se still goin', honey,
I'se still climbin',
And life for me ain't been no crystal stair.

landin's: landings, the level floors at the top or bottom of flights of stairs

Perseverance

Johann Wolfgang von Goethe

We must not hope to be mowers,
    And to gather the ripe gold ears,
Unless we have first been sowers
    And watered the furrows with tears.

It is not just as we take it,
    This mystical world of ours,
Life's field will yield as we make it
    A harvest of thorns or of flowers.

---

mowers: reapers; those who cut and gather the crop
sowers: those who plant seeds
furrows: the rows in a plowed field
mystical: having a hidden spiritual meaning
yield: to produce; to bear fruit

REBECCA
WHO SLAMMED DOORS FOR FUN AND PERISHED MISERABLY

Hilaire Belloc

A Trick that everyone abhors
In Little Girls is slamming Doors.
A Wealthy Banker's Little Daughter
Who lived in Palace Green, Bayswater
(By name Rebecca Offendort),
Was given to this Furious Sport.

She would deliberately go
And Slam the door like Billy-Ho!
To make her Uncle Jacob start.
She was not really bad at heart,
But only rather rude and wild;
She was an aggravating child...

It happened that a Marble Bust
Of Abraham was standing just
Above the Door this little Lamb
Had carefully prepared to Slam,
And Down it came! It knocked her flat!
It laid her out! She looked like that.

---

abhors: hates
deliberately: purposefully; intentionally
aggravating: annoying
bust: a sculpture showing a person's head, neck, and shoulders

Her funeral Sermon (which was long
And followed by a Sacred Song)
Mentioned her Virtues, it is true,
But dwelt upon her Vices too,
And showed the Dreadful End of One
Who goes and slams the door for Fun.

The children who were brought to hear
The awful Tale from far and near
Were much impressed, and inly swore
They never more would slam the Door,
—As often they had done before.

inly: inwardly

THE STORY OF AUGUSTUS
WHO WOULD NOT HAVE ANY SOUP

Heinrich Hoffmann

Augustus was a chubby lad;
Fat, ruddy cheeks Augustus had;
And everybody saw with joy
The plump and hearty, healthy boy.
He ate and drank as he was told,
And never let his soup get cold.

But one day, one cold winter's day,
He screamed out—"Take the soup away!
O take the nasty soup away!
I won't have any soup today."

Next day begins his tale of woes;
Quite lank and lean Augustus grows.
Yet, though he feels so weak and ill,
The naughty fellow cries out still—

"Not any soup for me, I say:
O take the nasty soup away!
I won't have any soup today."

The third day comes: O what a sin!
To make himself so pale and thin.
Yet, when the soup is put on table,
He screams as loud as he is able—

---

ruddy: rosy in color, as a sign of health
lank: thin

"Not any soup for me, I say:
O take the nasty soup away!
I WON'T have any soup today."

Look at him, now the fourth day's come!
He scarcely weighs a sugar-plum;
He's like a little bit of thread,
And on the fifth day, he was—dead!

sugar-plum: a small, ball-shaped candy

Index of Authors and Titles

ACKNOWLEDGMENTS

"Thank You, M'am" from SHORT STORIES by Langston Hughes. Copyright © 1996 by Ramona Bass and Arnold Rampersad. Reprinted by permission of Hill and Wang, a division of Farrar, Strauss, and Giroux, LLC.

"The Circuit" by Francisco Jiménez. Reprinted from *Arizona Quarterly* 28 (1972) by permission of Francisco Jiménez.

"The Bracelet" by Yoshiko Uchida. Copyright © 1976. Reprinted by permission of the Bancroft Library.

"Waiting" by Harry Behn from THE LITTLE RED HILL by Harry Behn. Copyright © 1949 by Harry Behn, copyright renewed 1977 by Alice L. Behn. Used by permission of Marian Reiner.

"Something Told the Wild Geese" by Rachel Field from POEMS by Rachel Field. Copyright © 1934 Macmillan Publishing Company; copyright renewed © 1962 by Arthur S. Pederson. Reprinted by permission of Simon and Schuster Books for Young Readers, an imprint of Simon and Schuster Children's Publishing Division.

Six Haiku from CRICKET SONGS: JAPANESE HAIKU translated or written by Harry Behn. Copyright © 1964 by Harry Behn, copyright renewed 1992 by Prescott Behn, Pamela Behn Adam and Peter Behn. Used by permission of Marian Reiner.

"The Storm" by Walter de la Mare, reprinted by permission of the Literary Trustees of Walter de la Mare and the Society of Authors as their representative.

"Until I Saw the Sea" by Lilian Moore from I FEEL THE SAME WAY by Lilian Moore. Copyright © 1966, 1967 by Lilian Moore. Used by permission of Marian Reiner for the author.

"Michael Faraday's World" adapted from COILS, MAGNETS AND RINGS: MICHAEL FARADAY'S WORLD by Nancy Veglahn, copyright © by Nancy Veglahn, text. Used by permission of Coward-McCann, a division of Penguin Young Readers Group, A Member of Penguin Group (USA) Inc., 345 Hudson St., New York, NY 10014. All rights reserved.

"Nikola Tesla, Inventor" by Shawn Lake, reprinted and adapted by permission of CRICKET magazine, October 2002, Vol. 30, No. 2, copyright © 2002 by Shawn Lake.

"Enrico Fermi: 'The Italian Navigator'" by Dorothy Haas from MEN OF SCIENCE by Dorothy Haas, copyright © 1959, copyright renewed 1987 by Random House, Inc. Used by permission of Golden Books, an imprint of Random House Children's Books, a division of Random House, Inc.